A Perfect Match

Susan Axbey

HEINEMANN ELT NEW WAVE READERS

1 Man of the match

It was the final: Sporting v Atletico. Maria Santana looked around her. She could see the blue and white colours of the Atletico supporters, but mostly it was a sea of red. Red jackets, red T-shirts and red scarves. She too was wearing a red Club Sporting cap.

'Come on, Sporting,' she shouted.

'Spor-ting, Spor-ting,' Maria's friends joined in.

Maria knew her parents, her brother and all her friends were watching the game on television at home. Everyone in Spain wanted to see the final between these two top basketball clubs.

'I'm sure we're going to win,' thought Maria. 'And if we win, we'll be champions for the first time. We will win. We must.'

Sporting had reached the final last year too, but then they had lost. Now they had another chance.

Maria turned to her friend, Angela. 'I know we can do it,' she said. 'We're going to make history.'

But the noise was so great that the two girls couldn't hear themselves speak. Maria loved it: the colours, the cheering crowds and most of all the game. She was a good player herself, for her age.

She was fifteen now. Nearly sixteen. People said she had talent. She hoped she would get into the Junior Women's squad next season. But now her thoughts were on the match.

It was very close. Sporting were losing by only one point: 81-82. The coach called a time-out and the players gathered round him. Maria and her friends were sitting just behind the players' bench so they could hear what he said.

'Right. We play man-to-man defence. Watch out for their number three. Stop him shooting. And we must start scoring faster. But don't take stupid shots. Look for Danny.'

The coach put his arm round the tall American player and looked up at him. 'Danny, we need you now. Give me a hundred percent.'

'OK, coach. You got it.'

Danny Carpenter had answered in English. He understood Spanish and he could speak it too. But in the excitement of the matches he sometimes spoke English. Anyway, in Spanish or in English, there was certainly no communication problem with his coach. He and Danny understood each other perfectly.

'Oh, come on,' prayed Maria. 'Come on.'

In her excitement, she dropped her programme. She picked it up and turned quickly to page six again. There was a loud cheer. The players were coming back on court. Maria closed the programme and put it in her bag. She did not want to lose it. It was a special souvenir programme with facts and figures for every player.

On page six, Maria had read:

'Danny Carpenter   - Position: Forward
                             - Height: 1m 95
                             - Weight: 97 kilos
                             - Age: 23
                             - Birthplace: Los Angeles, USA.'

Maria looked up at the clock. There were three minutes and twenty-two seconds left to play. Atletico passed the ball around but they couldn't find a chance to shoot. Then they made a bad pass. A Sporting player got the ball. He passed it quickly to Danny Carpenter. Danny jumped high into the air, towering above the other players. Just for a second, he seemed to stop still in mid-air. Then he slammed the ball into the net. Both hands on the rim of the basket. Two points.

'Car-pen-ter, Car-pen-ter!' roared the crowd.

'Dan-ny, Dan-ny!' screamed Maria.

The score was 83-82. For the first time in the match, Sporting were in the lead. When the American was playing at his best, he inspired the whole team.

The lead increased to 89-84. The Atletico coach called a time-out. They made a substitution. Atletico closed the gap a little: 89-86. Then Carpenter got the ball. He was a long, long way from the basket, but with time for a shot. It was a great one. Straight through the net. Swish. The ball didn't even touch the rim of the basket. Three points! The Sporting fans knew the game was won.

When the final buzzer sounded, Sporting had won 101-90. The crowd cheered madly. They waved their red scarves. The players slapped hands and hugged each other. Maria jumped up and down with joy. 'Dan-ny. Well done!' they screamed.

Danny smiled and waved back.

The coach turned to Danny. 'We've done it. We're champions. Now you must stay with the club, Danny. You must sign another contract for next season.'

'Let's not talk about it now, Coach. It's a big decision. I need time to think.'

Maria could hear people in the crowd talking about him.

'What a player! The American.'

'Top scorer. Man of the match.'

'He won the game for us.'

'Let's hope he stays with Club Sporting.'

'Two other clubs are offering him more money.'

'I read in the newspaper he may go back to the USA.'

'I read he's not happy here.'

'Well, he looks happy enough now.'

Of course, Danny Carpenter was happy. It was a great moment for him. For the first time he really felt he belonged at Sporting. Today everyone wanted to shake his hand and pat him on the back.

But it hadn't always been like this.

Danny was a foreigner in Spain. He was American and some people didn't like that. He was away from home. Away from his friends and family. Life wasn't easy.

Would he sign another contract with Sporting? Would he go back to the USA? Danny Carpenter didn't want to think about any of these questions now. Questions about the future must wait. He wanted to enjoy the present.

'Hey, man, we did it! We did it!' he yelled.

And he lifted the coach onto the shoulders of the other players. The crowd cheered and cheered.

'We are the champions. We are the champions,' sang Maria and Angela.

2 Tensions at home

'I'll be working late next week,' Luisa Santana told her husband. 'We're short of staff at the hospital.' She passed him the plates.

'I'll be late too,' said Federico. He was manager of the electrical factory now and had extra responsibilities.

'Roberto and Maria can make their own dinner next week,' said his wife.

'I wish we could spend more time with them.' Federico looked serious. 'But I suppose they'd rather be with their own friends.'

Luisa was silent. She loved their house with its small garden. They had worked hard for it. There were tensions in the family but Luisa thought it was better not to talk about them. Federico worried too much. Things would get better with time, she hoped.

She looked at her husband. 'Have we got bread on the table?' she asked. Federico nodded. 'Well, you can spend some more time with them now,' she smiled. 'Dinner's ready.'

Federico smiled back. 'Good,' he said. 'I'm hungry.'

'Maria!' he called.

Maria was upstairs in her bedroom. She was lying on the bed looking at her scrapbook. On the last page, there were reports of Sporting's famous victory over Atletico. She could still remember the excitement. What a wonderful match!

Maria looked up at the wall above her. It was covered with photographs, posters and souvenirs. There was a Boston Celtics programme. A friend had brought that back from America. There were three posters: Larry Bird, Magic Johnson, Michael Jordan. All top players. Larry Bird, Magic Johnson . . . She liked to say their names. She liked the sound of their names.

'Maria! It's on the table.'

'All right. Coming.'

But Maria didn't get up. Her eyes moved to a photograph. It showed a women's team. At the bottom, it said 'UCLA'. University of California Los Angeles. Perhaps one of the players was Danny Carpenter's sister.

'Oh, come on, Maria.' Roberto, her elder brother, was standing in the doorway. 'Everyone's waiting for you.'

'You should knock before you come into my room.'

'I did.'

'Well, I didn't hear you.' She followed Roberto downstairs to join their parents for dinner.

'Hi, Maria.' Paco, Roberto's closest friend, was there too. They both played the guitar and spent a lot of time together.

Roberto was three years older than his sister. They had always got on well together when they were children but now they had different friends and different interests. And these days he was always making fun of her. That was the trouble with her family. They did not take her seriously. Sometimes her parents treated her like a child.

Now her father was talking about Club Sporting. He had read in the newspaper that the American player, Carpenter, had signed a new contract with the club. But Maria already knew that Danny Carpenter had decided to stay with Sporting. She stopped listening.

After a few minutes, her mother turned to her and asked, 'Maria, what have you been doing all day up in your room?'

Then, of course, Roberto had to get involved. He laughed. 'She's been staring at the pictures on her wall, haven't you Maria?'

'Mind your own business.'

'They're all American, anyway.'

'So what? What's that got to do with anything?'

'Because I know who you like. What's his name? Woodcutter?'

Maria's face went red.

'He thinks he's such a big star. Well, I don't like him at all and I don't trust him.'

Maria's father could see that she was getting upset. 'All right, Roberto. That's enough.'

'But, Dad, I thought you didn't like Americans.'

'It's true that your mother and I don't always agree with US policies. But I have nothing against individual Americans. People are people. All over the world.'

'Anyway,' said Roberto, 'Maria and her basketball. It's an obsession.'

'What about you and your music? It's the same thing,' Maria answered angrily.

'No, it's not.'

'Yes, it is.'

'It isn't.'

Maria's mother tried to help. 'Come on, Roberto, you're not being fair.'

And Paco too wanted to make peace. 'Yes, Roberto, you're crazy about music - American music too.'

Maria's father wanted the last word. 'All right. Enough. If Maria wants to play basketball, that's fine. Just so long as it doesn't affect her school work. Just so long as she gets good grades this year.'

By now Maria had a lump in her throat. 'They all talk about me as if I wasn't here,' she thought. She could feel the tears coming to her eyes.

She jumped up from the table. 'Why don't you leave me alone? All of you. You don't understand anything.' She left the room and slammed the door behind her.

She wished she could escape now and go to the basketball court. When she was playing, it gave her such a beautiful feeling. It was hard to describe. Jumping for the ball, running past her opponents, making them look slow and then going up for the shot. Sometimes she felt as if she were flying. She knew the ball would go in. She felt that she could do anything in the world.

But her family didn't understand how she felt. 'No,' she thought bitterly, 'they'll never understand.'

Later, in her bedroom, Maria calmed down a little. She could hear Roberto and Paco practising on their guitars in the next room. Why was Roberto so horrible to her all the time? Finally, the sound of the guitars stopped. It was time for Paco to go home.

In the next room Paco was putting away his guitar. 'You're a bit hard on her, Roberto, you know,' he said.

'Maria? It's just a bit of fun. She's only a kid.'

'Maybe.'

As he walked past Maria's door, Paco called out softly, 'Bye, Maria.'

But Maria didn't answer. She was asleep.

The next morning Maria's mother ran upstairs. 'Maria, I think this is the letter you've been waiting for.' She held out a brown envelope.

Maria's heart jumped. She tore open the envelope, read the letter quickly and dropped it on the floor. Then she threw herself onto the bed and put the pillow over her head. She was shaking.

Her mother picked up the letter and began to read it. 'But that's wonderful. They want you. I knew you'd get in.'

The letter was from Sporting. They wanted Maria to join the Junior Women's squad for the coming season.

Maria took the pillow off her head, sat up and hugged her mother. 'I just want to scream and shout, but I'm afraid the neighbours will think you're murdering me!'

Her mother laughed. They read the letter again. 'Dates of training . . . matches: home and away . . . coach.' And then 'Team Adviser: Danny Carpenter.' Maria breathed in quickly.

The letter ended, 'Welcome to Sporting. We wish you a successful season.'

Maria picked up the pillow and threw it into the corner of the room. It landed in the wastepaper basket.

'Two points,' joked her mother. They both laughed again.

'Oh,' said Maria, 'I'm so happy.'

3 Keeping your balance

Maria liked the Junior Women's squad. They made her feel welcome from the very first day. Of course, there was a lot of competition between the girls. When they played a match, everyone wanted to be in the first five and no-one wanted to sit on the bench. But the competition was always fair and friendly. Their coach, Manolo, made sure of that.

Manolo had been with Sporting longer than anyone could remember. He was well-respected both in the club and by the people in the town. Maria's parents knew him quite well. Manolo's brother worked with Federico Santana at the factory. Many years ago, Manolo had played for the club until injury forced him to stop. His hair was white now, but you could see that he had once been an elegant and skilful player. Manolo enjoyed coaching. He was particularly good with the younger players. Once, after training, some of the Junior Women's squad were talking about him.

'He reminds me of my uncle,' said Maria. 'My favourite uncle.'

'Yes. Me too,' said Esperanza, one of the players. 'Manolo is everyone's favourite uncle.' They all laughed.

'Maybe,' said another, 'but this evening he was more like a general in the army.' The girls laughed again.

It was true. Manolo was a tough coach and he trained them hard. First, they worked on general fitness and stamina. Then they practised individual skills: shooting, marking and ball control. Finally, as a team, they worked out different moves for attack and defence. Maria found this part difficult sometimes. You really had to concentrate. One day, as the girls were working on their moves, Manolo stopped them. 'Look,' he said. 'Basketball is like chess. Physical chess. To be a good player you have to be intelligent as well as being a first-class, all-round athlete.'

Usually Maria loved training. She was learning and improving all the time. But this evening she wasn't playing well at all. In the practice game at the end of the training session she made two or three bad mistakes.

'That's enough for tonight, Maria,' said Manolo. 'Just sit out and watch for a while, please.'

'I'm sorry, Manolo,' said Maria. She went and sat away from the court in the middle of the spectator seats. She was watching the game but her head was in her hands. She felt very low.

'Hi.'

Maria looked up. It was Danny Carpenter. He came and sat beside her. Sometimes, like tonight, he came in without anyone noticing and just sat watching for a while. Once he had helped Manolo with the training. 'Danny's a clever player,' Manolo told the girls. 'He knows what's what.'

'Oh, hello,' said Maria. 'I didn't know you were here. I played so badly tonight. Did you see me?'

'Yeah. But I've watched you play before, Maria. I know you're a good player and you're getting better.'

'I didn't think you knew who I was.'

'Number five and number seven there.' Danny pointed to the court. 'They're your two key players. And the tall girl with the fair hair. Esperanza. She's a good player too. But she needs to work on her shot.'

Maria was surprised. Danny smiled. 'Oh, sure. I know you all,' he said.

Suddenly, Maria couldn't think of anything to say. The great Danny Carpenter. His accent was strange. It was funny the way he said her name. But she liked it. They watched the game in silence.

Then Danny asked, 'Something on your mind?'

'Nothing,' said Maria quickly. The game continued. Manolo was shouting his instructions to the players.

'You can talk about it if you want,' Danny said.

'It's my father,' Maria started. 'You see, my grades at school were really bad this month. He's furious about it. Now he says basketball is interfering with my studies. He says he'll stop me playing if I don't work harder. Then we had this terrible row last night and I walked out. I just can't talk to him any more.'

It all came out in a rush. Maria felt foolish. Her face was burning.

Danny just said, 'Yeah'. He continued watching the game. 'Yeah,' he said. 'Manolo's doing a good job here.'

Maria's eyes went back to the game too. After a few minutes, Danny spoke.

'When I was at college in LA, I lived and breathed basketball. I never studied at all and so, of course, I failed to graduate. But I wasn't worried. I thought - so what? I'm going to be a pro. A professional basketball player. With the Los Angeles Lakers. The top team in the land. I don't need a college diploma.' He paused. 'I had it all planned, you see.'

Danny looked at Maria. He sounded angry. His eyes were shining. Maria said nothing.

'But you know what?' he went on. She shook her head. 'The Lakers didn't want me. And suddenly I was left with nothing.'

Maria didn't know what to say. She wanted to help. Finally, she said, 'Well, you're a big star here.'

Danny laughed. 'Well, tell that to the Lakers!' he said. 'You know something, Maria? I like you. I like you a lot.' And he laughed again.

At that moment, Manolo blew the whistle long and hard. It was the end of the training session. The coach always had a few words with everyone at the end. He waved to Maria and Danny to join them on court. As they stood up, Danny looked down at Maria.

'Your father's right, you know,' he said.

Maria sighed. She was disappointed. She thought Danny would understand the way she felt about playing basketball.

'Unless you're smarter than he thinks.'

'What do you mean?' Maria didn't understand.

'Look. Play basketball. You love it. You're good. Okay. But work hard at school too. Get good grades. Show your father you can do both things. Then you won't have to choose. Do you think you can do that?'

Maria smiled. 'Yes. I can. And I will. Thanks, Danny. I'll show him.'

They went down onto the court. Manolo looked up as they came. 'Maria,' he said, 'you're not yourself today. Have you got a problem?'

'Yes, she has,' said Danny. They all looked at him. Maria's face went red. She didn't want everyone to know about their conversation. 'It's her jump shot,' Danny went on. 'Her technique isn't right. But I think we've sorted out the problem now. It's all a question of keeping your balance. Right, Maria?' He smiled at her.

'Right,' she agreed. 'And thanks, Danny.'

On her way home, Maria kept repeating to herself, 'Thanks, Danny. Thanks.'

And she could still hear his voice saying, 'Maria. I like you. I like you a lot.'

4   A lack of trust

Although the match was not for another three weeks, everyone was already talking about it. Every year Sporting Junior Women played Atletico for a special Challenge Cup. Manolo explained the arrangements for this year's match.

'This time it's an away match so we'll go in the minibus. Tip-off's at five pm so we'll leave here about midday. After the match, we'll go out for dinner and then we'll stay the night in a hotel. We travel back the next day, Sunday. Now last year we lost so I'm expecting a victory this year.' He smiled. 'Anyway, win or lose, it's a great weekend away and good experience for all of you.'

Certainly Maria, the youngest player in the squad, was looking forward to the match. As the day of the match came nearer, she got more and more excited. But then suddenly, a week before the match, something happened which seemed to spoil everything. Manolo had a heart attack. No-one could believe it. He was slim and very fit for his age. He didn't smoke or drink. It was a great shock to all the players. Fortunately, it was only a mild attack and he was expected to make a good recovery. But a shadow fell over the girls. Would they still be able to play the challenge match now? Who would be their coach? They waited for the club's decision.

Then the best possible solution was found. Danny Carpenter offered to drive the team to the match and to act as coach. He wasn't playing that weekend so he was free to go with the girls. Everyone was delighted. Maria rushed home to tell her parents the good news. She thought they would be pleased.

'Carpenter is going? And who else?' asked her father.

'No-one,' said Maria. 'Just us. The players.'

'But not you. You won't be going.'

'Oh, I will. I'm in the squad. Danny said.'

'You don't understand, Maria,' explained her mother. 'We can't allow you to go. You're too young.'

'But you said I could go.'

'That was before - when we thought you'd be with Manolo.'

Maria's father looked very serious. 'We are not letting you go away for the weekend with that American,' he said firmly.

'That American? You mean Danny?'

'You and he are becoming rather too friendly. And we don't think he's a suitable person to take ten young girls away for the weekend.'

'Women,' protested Maria. 'We're not girls.'

'Well, yes. That's part of the problem.'

'You mean you don't trust Danny? Or you don't trust me?'

'No, Maria,' said her mother. 'Well, yes. I don't know. I mean we don't know what he's like.'

'Well, I do. He's a wonderful, wonderful person.'

'He's much older than you.'

'He's twenty-three. But you're not making any sense. First you say I'm too young. Then you say he's too old. Why don't you like him? Is it because he's American? Or is it because he's black?'

By now, Roberto and Paco, who was there as usual, had come downstairs to see what all the shouting was about.

'Mum and Dad are right. You must listen to them, Maria,' said Roberto. 'I told you before not to trust him.'

'Oh, not you too. I'm ashamed to be part of this family.'

She turned towards her brother's friend. 'Tell them how wrong they are, Paco,' she cried. 'Surely you can see.'

But Roberto was glaring at his friend. Paco moved away. 'I'm

sorry, I can't interfere. This is a family matter. I'm sorry, Maria.' And with that Paco went out looking very unhappy.

'Maria,' said her father. 'That's enough. Right or wrong, you have to do what we say. Tomorrow you must tell the club you're not going to the match.'

'I'll never ever forgive you for this. Never!' cried Maria. She ran upstairs to her bedroom and slammed the door.

Maria threw herself onto the bed and wept. She cried until no more tears could come. Then she

began to think about the match. She had to play in it. But how? She couldn't possibly tell Danny what her parents had said. She would be too ashamed. And she couldn't tell the other players either. They would laugh at her. Gradually a plan began to form in her mind. 'Yes,' she thought, 'that's what I'll do. They'll never find out.'

In the morning Maria came down to breakfast with red eyes. Her mother was making coffee. 'Maria,' she said, 'we're only trying to do what's best for you. When you're older you can do whatever you like. But now you must do what we want.'

'Even when you're wrong?' said Maria bitterly.

'One day you'll understand,' answered her mother sadly.

'I'll never understand,' replied Maria. 'But if I'm not going, then I'm not going.' She paused. 'And I don't want to talk about it any more.'

Her father had come in. 'Good,' he said. 'I think we all said too much last night. I'm sorry if we upset you but . . . '

'I don't want to talk about it, Dad.'

Maria poured herself some coffee, picked up a magazine and pretended to read. Her parents looked at each other. Both knew it was better not to say anything more. They went out of the kitchen together and left Maria alone.

5 Secret plans

The match was not mentioned again at home. Of course, Maria didn't tell Danny or any of the other players about what her parents had said. But over the next few days, she made her plans. One evening when her parents and Roberto were all out, she telephoned her friend, Angela, and told her what had happened.

'You've got to help me, Angela,' she said.

Their parents had been neighbours for many years and the two girls had grown up together. But now they lived in different parts of the city and went to different schools so they didn't see each other very often. But Angela was a loyal friend.

'Of course I'll help, Maria,' she said. 'What do you want me to do?'

'I want you to invite me to stay for the weekend.'

'Sure. It'll be great to see you again.'

'No, stupid. I'm not really going to come and stay. But I want you to pretend to my parents that you're inviting me,' explained Maria.

'Oh, I see. And what about my parents?' asked Angela.

'Don't say anything to them. As long as your parents don't talk to mine, no-one will ever find out. Okay?'

'Yes. Fine. When shall I phone?'

'Tomorrow evening. They'll be in then. And try to sound natural. I'm sure they won't suspect anything.'

Maria was right. When Angela phoned with the invitation, her parents were pleased. They thought that if she was away from home, enjoying herself with a friend, she would forget about the basketball match.

'So far, so good,' thought Maria. 'Well done, Angela.'

Saturday came. Maria was up early. She took down her overnight bag. She put her basketball boots and her kit into it. She spread her towel on top and then added other things she needed for an overnight stay. When she left home, Maria told her mother she would walk to the station and then catch a train. Angela would meet her at the other end.

'Are you sure you wouldn't like me to drive you over to Angela's?' her mother offered.

'No, Mum. It's all right really,' said Maria. 'I'll go by train. Thanks all the same.'

'Well, enjoy yourself then. See you tomorrow. And give our best wishes to Angela's parents.'

Maria hadn't lied about everything. She was going to the station. That was where the team had arranged to meet Danny.

When she arrived, the other girls were already there. 'Hi, Maria,' they shouted.

'Okay,' said Danny. 'Is everyone here? Let's go.'

They all climbed into the minibus laughing and talking excitedly. As Danny drove away, some of the girls started to sing.

Danny noticed that Maria was very quiet. She seemed to be looking for something out of the window. She looked worried.

'She must be nervous before the big match,' he thought. 'Funny kid. Reminds me a bit of my sister.'

But after about half an hour, Maria began to relax and joined in talking and joking with the others. They were out of the city now and a long way from home.

It was a fine day and Maria's parents were in the garden but they couldn't relax.

'Perhaps we've done the wrong thing, Federico,' said Maria's mother. 'It's terrible to lose your daughter's trust.'

'Yes,' her husband replied. 'I'm worried about that too. Maria hardly speaks to me any more. But, you know, Luisa, it's better to be safe than sorry. The world's a dangerous place and she doesn't really understand that yet.'

'Well, I just hope we've done the right thing. She's looked so miserable these last few days,' said Maria's mother. 'I think I'll just phone Angela to see if she's arrived. I'd like to hear Maria sounding more cheerful.'

Luisa Santana went into the house to telephone. She came back in a few minutes and told her husband that she'd spoken to Angela and everything was all right. Maria had arrived safely. The girls were just going out to meet some friends. They were in a hurry. So Maria's mother agreed to phone again later to have a word with her daughter.

Two hours later Maria's mother picked up the phone and dialled Angela's number. But this time, Angela's mother was sitting next to the phone. She picked it up and answered before her daughter could reach it.

'Oh no, Luisa, we haven't seen Maria for months.'

It didn't take long for the truth to come out. Maria's mother was surprised and upset. Angela's mother was amazed and then angry. Angela didn't know what to say. She finally broke down and confessed.

Maria's parents were shocked. Their emotions were confused: anger, fear, regret, anxiety. They didn't know what to think. For a few moments, they just sat and stared at each other, not speaking. Then her mother stood up. 'We must find her, Federico,' she exclaimed. 'We must make sure she's all right.'

'Perhaps she didn't go to the match, Luisa. Perhaps she's run away from home.' Maria's father was beginning to panic.

'We must keep calm, Federico,' said his wife. 'I'm sure she's gone to the match.' She ran upstairs to Maria's bedroom. 'Yes. Her basketball things have gone.'

Roberto and Paco were playing their guitars but Roberto had heard his mother's voice and stopped. The two boys came to see what had happened.

'Roberto, Maria's gone to the basketball match. You'll have to go after her. Here's some money for the train. Go now and phone us as soon as you have any news,' said his mother. 'I'm going over to talk to Angela and your father will stay here in case Maria phones.'

'Oh, no,' complained Roberto. 'Paco and I were just going out to a concert.'

'Well, you can't. This is important, Roberto.' She turned to Paco. 'I'm sorry about this, Paco.'

'Go on, Roberto. Do what your mother says,' his father pleaded. 'Please,' he added weakly.

Roberto had never seen his father like this before. His face was quite grey.

'I hope she's all right,' Paco said as Roberto left.

'Of course she's all right,' Roberto thought to himself as he sat on the train some time later. 'A lot of fuss about nothing. That stupid sister of mine. Now I've missed the concert. It's all her fault. I'll kill her.'

As the train passed through the suburbs of the city, Roberto began to think about Danny Carpenter. 'I wonder what's going on between Maria and that American. I hope he hasn't touched her. If he has, I'll kill him too.'

Roberto thought about the concert. Had Paco gone on his own or had he found someone else to go with? 'My sister!' he thought angrily. 'She's spoilt my whole weekend.'

6 A Face in the crowd

Maria was nervous at first. It was a strange court and there were no Sporting supporters there. But she soon relaxed and started to play well. The whole team were playing well and the girls began to feel very confident. But this was dangerous. Sporting had led from the beginning of the match, but now Atletico were gradually closing the gap. The score was 32-28 to Sporting. Then one of the Sporting players was careless. An Atletico player grabbed the ball. She was a tall girl and very fast. The Sporting defence were slow to get back and she had an easy shot. Then almost immediately the same thing happened again. Another easy lay-up. Now the score was even: 32-32. The Atletico supporters cheered. Danny called a time-out.

'Look. You've been playing well but now you're just giving the points away.' The girls could see that he was annoyed with them. 'Now come on, we've got three minutes to go before half-time.'

Maria reached for a towel to wipe her face. As she threw the towel down again, something made her look up at the spectators sitting behind the bench. To her surprise and horror, she saw her brother Roberto's face in the crowd. Their eyes met. Roberto looked very serious and very angry. Maria's heart stopped. Panic swept over her.

'We'll keep to the zone defence,' Danny continued. 'But you've got to concentrate. Okay. Let's go. One, two, three - defence!'

'Defence!' answered the players and they went back on court determined not to let Atletico score again. But Maria's hands were trembling and when the ball came to her, she dropped it. She turned and ran back to collect the ball. She was usually so fast but now her legs felt as heavy as lead. An Atletico player ran past her, got the ball and had an easy shot. 32-34. Sporting were losing for the first time in the match. The whistle went for half-time. Maria came off the court with her head down.

'What's the matter, Maria? Are you ill?' Danny asked urgently.

She looked up to where Roberto had been sitting. The seat was empty but his jacket was still there. There was no escape. He had found her. He would be waiting for her after the match. Were her parents there too? No. They had probably sent Roberto to find her by himself. She would have to face him first and then her parents later.

'What's wrong? What is it?'

She turned to Danny. He looked concerned. She couldn't speak and the tears rolled silently down her cheeks.

'Come on, Maria. I can't help you if you don't tell me.'

'I had a row with my parents,' she managed to say.

'But I thought your grades at school were much better now?'

'It's not that. I didn't want to tell you about it. Couldn't. But now my brother's here. And . . .'

The tears came again but Maria continued with her story. Danny soon understood what had happened. He didn't have time to think about the rights and wrongs of it all now. Somehow he had to find a way to get through to Maria quickly. He had to make her forget all her problems and just concentrate on the match.

Danny held her by the shoulders, looked her straight in the eye and spoke in a low, quiet voice. 'Okay, Maria, so you're in a mess. So you've got problems. They're not going to go away. They're going to be waiting for you after the game.'

Maria looked down at the ground.

'But right now, you've got the chance to do something beautiful. Remember that feeling you told me about? Like flying, you said.'

She looked up and tried to smile. Danny wiped a tear from her cheek.

'Well, come on - show the people how you can fly. It's magic, you know. A lot of people would like to see that.' Danny laughed. 'Hey - a young lady flying around a basketball court! What do you think of that?'

Maria made a funny sound in her throat. She wanted to laugh, but she couldn't.

'That's better,' Danny said. 'Now you can do it. I told Manolo you'd be my star player. So don't let me down. Do it for me, Maria. And do it for the team.'

Maria nodded. She wiped her face on her towel and turned away from Danny. She joined the other players.

'Hey,' Danny called after her softly. 'Hey - do it for yourself.'

The other players never knew what Danny said to her. But they soon realised that when Maria came back on court after half-time she was all right again. She was more than all right. She was brilliant. Sporting regained the lead and Atletico could not get back. Maria was everywhere, working tirelessly both in defence and attack. No-one could stop her. She didn't miss a shot. She was flying. When the final whistle blew, Sporting had won by eight points: 64-56.

The rest of the team ran to Maria to congratulate her. More than any other player, she had helped them to win. They all knew that. The Atletico supporters knew it too.

'Number four. What a good game she's had!' one of them said.
'Actually, she's my sister,' Roberto told him.
'Really? You must be very proud of her.'
But Roberto wasn't proud of her. He couldn't enjoy his sister's success. He had seen Danny Carpenter holding Maria by the shoulders at half-time. He had seen the way he talked to her. Once, Carpenter had touched her face with his hand. How intimate were they? His parents were right. What did they really know about this stranger from another country who seemed to be so close to his sister?

After the match, the Sporting team went back to the hotel to relax and then get ready for dinner at a nearby restaurant. They would celebrate their victory there. Some of the players had already telephoned friends and family to tell them the result.

Roberto too had phoned home. But that was just to tell his parents that he had found Maria. He told them that he would stay overnight and then come back with her tomorrow. Neither Roberto nor his parents mentioned the game.

It couldn't be avoided any longer. Danny, Roberto and Maria finally had to sit down together to talk. They met in the lounge of the hotel. The meeting was even worse than Maria had imagined.

At first, Roberto didn't give either Danny or Maria a chance to speak. 'Who do you think you are? You people,' he raged, 'you come to our country. Take our money. And then you think you can have our women too. You made my sister cheat and lie to her parents. So that she could be with you.'

'Roberto, you don't understand. You don't know what you're talking about. He didn't know anything about it,' cried Maria. 'It was my idea.'

But it was too late. Danny didn't understand everything Roberto said. But he know Roberto was insulting him. That was clear.

'And you people,' responded Danny angrily. 'What are you? You have small minds. You have sad prejudices. I'm sorry for your sister. To have a brother like you.'

Maria stared at the floor in desperation. She was afraid they would fight, but Danny got up and walked out of the room. Roberto calmed down.

'Are you all right, Maria?' he asked.

'Oh, shut up, Roberto. You've said enough today.' She stood up and took the lift upstairs to her room.

At last, Maria was alone with her thoughts. Danny and Roberto were so far apart. And yet she was close to them both. So why did they have to be enemies? Danny and Roberto didn't even try to understand the other's point of view. Then she remembered her own angry scenes with her parents. Had she tried to understand their point of view? Probably not.

She wasn't sure of anything any more. Sadly, Maria got dressed and went back down to the hotel lounge to meet the others for dinner.

7 Just a Little blood

At the restaurant, everyone sat together at a long table. Roberto had joined them and he was sitting next to Maria in the middle of the table. She introduced him to Esperanza who was on his right and to the girls sitting opposite him. They knew a friend of Roberto's and so the conversation soon went along happily enough. Maria was relieved. She turned her back on her brother and joined in the conversation with the group at the end of the table. They were laughing and joking and talking about the match. Maria began to relax a little. Anyway, things were now moving out of her control. There was nothing she could do and she felt strangely light-hearted. She might as well enjoy herself. At the far end of the table, Danny was talking to two of the players who had spent most of the match on the bench. He was being really nice to them. 'You only played for a few minutes today,' Maria heard him say. 'But you did well. Your chance will come.'

In this way, Danny, Roberto and Maria got through the meal. There was still tension between them but they managed to hide this so that it didn't spoil the celebration for the others.

As they came out of the restaurant into the dark street, Maria shivered. It was late but fortunately the hotel was only a short walk away.

'Okay. Keep together, everyone,' said Danny. 'We'll soon be back and you can all get the sleep you deserve.'

Maria, Esperanza and some of the other girls were walking in front. Danny was behind them. Roberto had moved up and was now walking alongside Danny but they didn't speak to each other. Then Maria and her friends became aware of a group of young men standing at a street corner just ahead of them. The girls could hear voices and, as they drew nearer, one of the young men whistled. The others laughed. Roberto broke the silence between himself and Danny.

'Look at those men,' he said. 'They're bothering the girls.'

'I've already seen them,' answered Danny. 'Don't worry. The girls are sensible. They won't respond.'

Danny was right. Maria and her friends pretended not to notice the men. The girls spoke together very quietly and walked straight ahead. Danny and Roberto moved a little quicker. They could see the men clearly now. There were four of them. They were all young. One was wearing a blue jacket and he seemed to be the leader.

'I don't like the look of them,' said Roberto.

The best thing to do is to keep cool,' advised Danny.

Then two of the men stepped into the girls' path and blocked their way. Maria and the others were forced to stop. They were a little frightened but they stayed very calm. By now the men had seen Danny and Roberto approaching. When they saw Danny, they started to laugh and make rude comments. 'Yankee, yankee,' they jeered. 'Get out of our country.' Then they moved closer. 'Black dirt,' said the man in the blue jacket and he spat at Danny's feet.

Danny didn't react. All his life people had tried to start fights with him. It was strange. He was so much bigger and stronger than most people. But he'd got used to it. And the insults didn't bother him either. He had been called names before. 'Let them have their fun,' he thought. 'They'll soon get tired of it.'

All the time, Danny was watching Maria and the girls in front. So was Roberto. But Roberto was getting angry. He didn't like the way the man in the blue jacket was looking at Maria.

Danny sensed his anger. 'Keep cool, Roberto,' he warned.

But at that moment, the man smiled and tried to put his arm round Maria. She moved away. 'I like the sporty type,' he said nastily and his friends laughed. That was too much for Roberto.

'Leave my sister alone,' he yelled and pushed his way past Danny to face the man.

Then everything happened very fast. One of the men grabbed Roberto's arms and held them behind his back. The one in the blue jacket pulled out a knife. He had forgotten all about Maria now. The blade shone in the dim street lights. One of the girls screamed. Roberto struggled and managed to get one arm free. He shouted insults at the man in the blue jacket.

'You fool,' thought Danny. He could see what was coming. And as the knife swung upwards towards Roberto's face, he moved like lightning and grabbed the man's hand. There was a cry of pain and the knife fell to the ground. Roberto had his hand over his face. There was blood running through his fingers. Still holding the man with one hand, Danny bent down and picked up the knife. He held it against the man's throat. The other men had run away as soon as they saw Danny move. Knowing he was on  his own, the man in the blue jacket stared into Danny's face. His eyes were full of fear. Danny stared back at him. For a moment, he was ready to cut the man's throat. Then he shook his head, sighed and let go of him. The man fell to the ground, too terrified to move. His blue jacket was covered in dirt.

'Okay, everyone, it's all over,' said Danny. 'Nothing to worry about. Let's get back to the hotel.'

Then he turned to look at Roberto whose face was covered with blood. But only his hand had been cut. Danny had stopped the man just in time. Maria gave her brother a scarf to wrap around his hand.

'Oh, Roberto,' she said. 'You might have been killed.'

'Yeah,' said Danny, giving him a long, hard look. 'Just a little blood this time. But if you want to stay alive much longer, you'd better learn to keep cool.'

Roberto looked down at his bleeding hand. 'I know,' he mumbled. 'I'm sorry.'

Then he looked up at Danny. 'And thanks. Thanks for saving my life.'

8 Like Old friends

It was difficult for Roberto. He had been suspicious of Danny. He had accused him of all kinds of things with no reason and with no proof. He had said terrible things to him. Now Danny had saved his life. And probably saved Maria too.

It had been a frightening situation. He and Danny alone against those four young men. But how different their reactions had been. Panic and stupidity. That had been him. Then courage and quiet self-control. That had been Danny. Roberto was full of admiration for Danny now. But what did Danny think of him? Roberto didn't like to think about this.

Sunday morning. Everyone was ready for the journey back. So much had happened in twenty-four hours. They felt they had been away from home for a very long time. The team began to climb into the back of the minibus. Danny sat in the driver's seat and asked Roberto to sit in the front beside him.

Roberto lifted up his bandaged hand. 'I don't know how to thank you,' he said.

Danny didn't say anything. He was very relieved that he'd managed to get the girls home safely last night. It had been an ugly situation and he knew he'd been lucky. Sometimes he worried about himself. It was easy to hate. He was strong but sometimes he was afraid of his own strength. It was difficult to keep control all the time. One day he might really use his strength and hurt someone.

But he kept these thoughts to himself. Then he saw that Roberto had offered his hand. His good hand.

'It's nothing,' said Danny. He shook Roberto's hand. He grinned at him. 'I've seen a lot worse things in LA,' he said.

Roberto smiled back. Was it possible? Could they become friends after such a bad start?

Danny started up the minibus and they drove off.

'Tell me about it,' said Roberto. 'Los Angeles. What's it really like?'

They talked. Danny told Roberto about Los Angeles. His family weren't poor. They were well-educated professional people. His father was an engineer, his mother a doctor. They wanted their son to have a good education and career too. But as a teenager Danny had rebelled and for a year or two he had joined a street gang.

'I saw the tough side of LA then but luckily I fell in love with basketball before I got into any real trouble. It didn't do much for my education but it sure kept me off the streets,' he laughed.

Roberto talked about music. About the ambitions he and Paco had. Next month they were planning to make a demo tape and send it to the record companies. Danny had brought some cassettes with him and Roberto found they liked the same kind of music.

Maria watched them talking. She was pleased to see that they were getting on so well. Perhaps that would help when they got home and she had to face her parents. She wasn't looking forward to that.

Her team-mates had been very kind when she told them her story. 'All families have rows,' they said.

'But you don't know my parents,' said Maria. 'My father can be so stubborn.'

'Oh, so that's where you get it from,' one joked and even Maria had to laugh. Then the others began telling stories of arguments they had had with their families. Sometimes their parents sounded very much like hers. She began to realise that her family was not so different after all. In fact, when Esperanza told them a story about her father, Maria thought to herself, 'But that's awful. My father would never say that to me.' And she thought how open and honest her father was. She remembered too the good fun they used to have together a few years ago. He was not so bad after all. She looked at Roberto sitting in the front. He and Danny were sharing a joke. Perhaps her brother was not so bad either.

What were they saying to each other? She tried to listen.

'But the terrible things people do,' Roberto was saying. 'I don't know how you can laugh at them like that.'

'Well, you either laugh or cry,' replied Danny. 'I've learned to laugh.'

'But it must be difficult being a foreigner here,' Roberto went on. 'And because you're -'

'Black.' Danny finished the sentence for him. 'Look. Most people I meet here are fine. Just fine.' Then he explained, 'If some people don't like me, I figure it's their problem. Not mine.'

Roberto thought about that for a while.

Then he asked, 'Don't you get lonely sometimes?'

Maria was amazed to hear Roberto and Danny talking like this about such things. They sounded like old friends.

'Yeah, sometimes,' Danny admitted. 'I miss my girlfriend a lot.'

Maria felt her heart jump. She had never heard Danny talk about a girlfriend before. But why did she feel so shocked?

'Is she in Los Angeles?' Roberto asked.

'Yeah. She's finishing college soon,' Danny went on. 'Then she's coming here to join me.'

Maria reminded herself that Danny was twenty-three. Of course he would have a girlfriend. Why had she never thought of that before? Suddenly, she felt very foolish. She felt like a child. Luckily, she had kept her daydreams to herself. She had never told anyone how she had sometimes imagined Danny and herself walking hand in hand together. Sharing things together. 'Well,' she thought, swallowing hard. 'That's my secret. It was only a daydream anyway.'

'Wake up, Maria,' Esperanza said. 'We're here.'

They all began to get out. 'Good luck with your parents, Maria,' the other girls said. 'Everything will be all right, you'll see.'

'Well done, all of you,' said Danny. 'You were great. You deserved to win. Manolo's going to be real proud of you when I tell him about the match.'

'Thanks for coming with us, Danny.'

'That's okay. Don't forget training on Tuesday as usual.'

The girls waved their goodbyes. Then Danny turned to Roberto and Maria who were standing beside the bus.

'Well, Maria,' he said. 'Are you ready to face the music at home?' He patted Roberto on the shoulder. 'And Roberto, will you give your sister some support for a change?' He smiled at them both.

'Why don't you come home with us?' asked Roberto. 'I'd like you to meet our parents after all that's happened.'

'Yes, please come with us,' Maria added.

'Yeah. Sure. Maybe that's a good idea.' Danny grinned again. 'I don't want them to think that I ran away with their daughter and then tried to kill their son!'

Both Roberto and Maria went a little red. Then they all three laughed. As they walked the short distance to the house, each of them was secretly feeling a little nervous.

9 Seeing with new eyes

When the three of them walked through the door, Maria's parents hardly noticed Danny and they totally ignored Maria. Instead, they took one look at Roberto's bandaged hand and then gave him all their attention. They were so worried. What had happened? How? Was it broken? When? Where? Was he hurt anywhere else? Roberto led his parents out into the garden to tell them the whole story. Danny and Maria were left alone in the sitting room.

'It's funny,' said Maria. 'I was expecting them to be so angry with me because of the way I deceived them. But I think they've forgotten all about me now.'

'Oh, no, we haven't,' said her father as he came into the room. 'You shouldn't have lied to us. But perhaps we were partly to blame ourselves.' He put his arm around Maria. 'We'll talk about it another time. All right?'

'Okay,' agreed Maria. But her father was smiling and she knew that everything would be all right between them now.

Her father turned to Danny. He looked very serious. 'I have two things I'd like to say to you, young man,' he began.

Maria began to feel nervous again. But she need not have worried.

'First of all,' her father went on. 'I want to apologise for not trusting you before. I should have invited you to our house and tried to get to know you. I was in the wrong. I'm sorry.'

Danny did not know what to say to Federico Santana's little speech. He was embarrassed. He wished he could escape but he couldn't run out of the room now. He smiled politely.

'And secondly,' Maria's father continued. 'I want to thank you for saving my son's life. For that, I can never repay you.'

'Yeah. Well, I . . .' Danny was lost for words. This was all much too emotional for him. Now the whole family were standing in the middle of the room looking uncomfortable. They weren't used to such serious talk. Finally, Maria's mother came to everyone's rescue.

'Why don't we all have lunch?' she suggested. 'There's plenty to eat and I'm sure you must be hungry.'

Immediately everyone began to relax. Danny sat down with Maria's father and they started chatting.

'Roberto, come and give me a hand with the food,' his mother said. 'And Maria, go and get Paco.'

'Paco?' said Maria.

'Yes. He's upstairs. Trying not to interfere in our family matters.' Roberto laughed.

'But he *is* family,' said Maria and she ran upstairs to find him. Of course, he was in Roberto's room playing the guitar. Today he was singing too. Maria stopped outside the door. It was a lovely melody. She liked it. It was a song about 'a girl with beautiful eyes'.

'But she doesn't see me. She doesn't see me,' sang Paco.

Maria opened the door quietly. Paco was sitting by the window with his back to her. He kept on singing. And then he sensed that someone else was in the room. He stopped and turned round.

'Oh, it's you,' he said. His face went red.

'It's such a lovely song,' said Maria. 'I've never heard it before.'

'I wrote it,' admitted Paco.

'Did you? It's lovely.'

'It's you, Maria,' he said. 'I wrote it about you. For you.'

'Oh.'

Now Maria's face went red. She couldn't think what to say. Paco. He was always there. He was always on her side. And his song was

true. She had never really looked at him properly before. Paco stood up. He was taller than Roberto. But not as tall as Danny, of course. He came towards her. 'He's quite good-looking,' she thought. 'Nice eyes.' Then she remembered the song and blushed again.

'Well, lunch is ready,' said Maria desperately.

Paco was still holding his guitar. He put it down. There was another awkward silence. Maria suddenly felt weak. She thought she might burst into tears. She couldn't think why.

'What about the match?' Paco asked. 'Did you win?'

It was just the right thing to say. Maria suddenly realised that Paco understood her better than anyone else in the world. She looked at him and smiled.

'She does see, you know,' she said.

Paco took Maria's hand and they went downstairs together.

STORY POINTS

Chapter 1
1. Why does everyone want to see this Sporting - Atletico match?
2. What is Maria's personal ambition?
3. Why does the Sporting coach say, 'Danny, we need you now.'?

Chapter 2
4. Why doesn't Maria hear her parents calling her?
5. What does Roberto do and say to upset Maria?
6. Why is Maria happy at the end?

Chapter 3
7. Describe Manolo, the coach.
8. Why isn't Maria playing well this evening?

Chapter 4
9. Why do Maria's parents change their minds about allowing her to play in the away match?
10. Does Maria accept her parents' decision?

Chapter 5
11. What is Maria's secret plan?
12. How do Maria's parents feel when they realise what she has done?
13. Why is Roberto angry?

Chapter 6
14. Why does Maria suddenly start to play badly just before half time?
15. Which of the words below best describes the meeting between Danny and Roberto?
conversation argument discussion chat row fight disagreement

Chapter 7
16. How do Maria, Danny and Roberto behave during the meal?
17. How does Danny save Roberto's life?

Chapter 8
18. What do Danny and Roberto talk about on the journey home?
19. What is Maria's secret daydream?

Chapter 9
20. Are Maria's parents still angry with her?
21. How does Paco feel about Maria?
22. What does Maria realise in the end?